SAKA – FOOTBALL AND LIFE

Inside the World of True Fans

By Pitt Anddy

© Copyright 2024 - All rights reserved.

The content contained within this book may not be reproduced, duplicated, or transmitted without direct written permission from the author or the publisher. Under no circumstances will any blame or legal responsibility be held against the publisher or author for any damages, repercussions, or monetary loss due to the information contained within this book, either directly or indirectly. You are responsible for your own choices, actions, and results.

Legal Disclaimer: This book is copyrighted. This book is strictly for personal use only. Without the author's or publisher's permission, you may not change, distribute, sell, use, quote, or paraphrase any of the content in this book.

Disclaimer Notice: Please note the information contained within this document is for educational and entertainment purposes only. All effort has been executed to present accurate, up to date, and reliable, complete information. No warranties of any kind are declared or implied. Readers acknowledge that the author is not engaging in the rendering of legal, financial, medical, or professional advice.

The content within this book has been derived from various sources. Please consulta licensed professional before attempting any techniques outlined in this book. By reading this document, the reader agrees that under no circumstances is the author responsible for any losses, direct or indirect, which are incurred as a result of the use of the information contained within this document, including, but not limited to, errors, omissions, or inaccuracies.

INTRODUCTION

"Saka - Football And Life" invites you to dig into the compelling story of Bukayo Saka, a rising star among Arsenal FC's ranks. This well researched and incisive book dives into the life and career of the young English midfielder, charting his incredible rise from humble origins to a vital role in the Premier League.

This book contains undiscovered experiences, remarkable meetings, and key moments that moulded Bukayo Saka's professional and personal development. From his early days to his quick rise in professional football, the book highlights the attributes that have garnered him the adoration of fans and experts alike.

Featuring extensive interviews, compelling visuals, and comprehensive analysis, "Saka – Football And Life" offers an intimate glimpse into the player's life. Whether you're a devoted fan or a football enthusiast, this book provides a thorough exploration of one of the sport's most promising talents.

Take a journey into the heart of Bukayo Saka's football identity, his everlasting passion, and the goals that drive him to success on the pitch. "Saka - Football And Life" honours his developing career, leaving an unforgettable impression in the world of sport..

HOW TO USE AUGMENTED REALITY (AR) TECHNOLOGY IN THIS BOOK

SCAN QR CODE

STEP 1 – Open camera & scan the QR code.

ACCESS AR PAGE

STEP 2 - See what else in this book comes to life when you scan it.

TABLE OF CONTENTS

INTRODUCTION 4

PERSONAL LIFE 9

CLUB CAREER 18

NATIONAL TEAM CAREER 27

RECORDS AND PERSONAL
ACHIEVEMENTS 38

TECHNIQUE AND PLAYING STYLE 44

DO YOU WANT TO MEET BUKAYO SAKA IN YOUR OWN SPACE?

Please scan the **QR code** to experience the **augmented reality (AR)** technology integrated into this book.

PERSONAL LIFE

- ⚽ Nigerian Heritage: Bukayo Saka's parents are originally from Nigeria, which is why he has strong connections to his Nigerian heritage despite being born in the UK.
- ⚽ Family-Oriented: Despite his fame and success, Saka continues to live with his parents, emphasizing his close-knit family values and upbringing.

- Religion: He is a devout Christian, often attributing his success and resilience to his faith.
- Education: Saka was an A* student in school, demonstrating intelligence and a strong work ethic from an early age.
- Home Life: His home environment is said to be supportive and grounding, with his family instilling a

sense of humility and hard work.

- ⚽ Early Football Influences: Saka's football journey started at a young age, influenced by his father's passion for the sport.
- ⚽ Role Model: He cites Thierry Henry as one of his footballing idols, indicating his admiration for Arsenal's greats.

- ⚽ Community Engagement: Saka is known for his involvement in community projects and charity work, reflecting his commitment to giving back.
- ⚽ Personality: He is described as humble and down-to-earth by teammates and coaches, maintaining a positive attitude despite his success.

- ⚽   Hobbies and Interests: Apart from football, Saka enjoys playing video games and listening to music in his spare time.
- ⚽   Strong Work Ethic: He has a reputation for being one of the hardest-working players at Arsenal, always putting in extra training hours.
- ⚽   Relationship with Teammates: Saka has built strong relationships with his

Arsenal teammates, who regard him as a friendly and approachable individual.

- Ambition: Saka has a strong drive to succeed, aiming to be one of the best players in the world and achieve significant milestones in his career.
- Charitable Work: He is involved in various charity projects, showing his desire to

use his platform to make a positive impact on society.

- ⚽ Influence on Youth: Saka is seen as a role model for young footballers, often inspiring them to work hard and follow their dreams.
- ⚽ Strong Arsenal Ties: Having been with Arsenal since his youth, Saka has deep connections to the club and its traditions.

- ⚽ Music Preferences: He enjoys listening to a variety of music genres, which he uses to relax and unwind.
- ⚽ Positive Mindset: Saka is known for his optimistic outlook on life, often approaching challenges with a can-do attitude.
- ⚽ Leadership Qualities: Despite his young age, Saka has shown leadership skills on

the pitch, often guiding and motivating his teammates.

⚽   Recognition and Awards: Saka has received various accolades for his performances, highlighting his growing influence and talent in the football world.

CLUB CAREER

- ⚽ Hale End Academy Product: Bukayo Saka joined Arsenal's Hale End Academy at the age of 8, marking the beginning of his journey with the club.
- ⚽ First-Team Debut: He made his first-team debut for Arsenal at just 17 years old, under the management of Unai Emery.

⚽ Versatile Player: Saka has played in various positions, including left-back, left-wing, and right-wing, showcasing his versatility.

⚽ FA Cup Winner: Saka was part of the Arsenal squad that won the FA Cup in the 2019-2020 season, a significant achievement early in his career.

⚽ Community Shield Success: He also won two FA

Community Shields with Arsenal, in 2020 and 2023, adding to his list of honours.

- Breakout Season: Saka's breakout season came in 2019-2020 when he began to establish himself as a key player in Arsenal's first team.
- Player of the Season: In 2020-2021, Saka was named Arsenal's Player of the Season, underlining his impact on the team.

- ⚽ **Consistent Performer:** Saka's consistency on the field has made him one of Arsenal's most reliable players, earning him a regular starting position.
- ⚽ **Contract Extension:** Arsenal secured Saka's future by signing him to a long-term contract extension in 2020, demonstrating their faith in his talent.

- ⚽ Youngest Arsenal Player: Saka holds the record for being the youngest Arsenal player to start a Premier League match at 17 years and 65 days old.
- ⚽ Assists Leader: During the 2019-2020 season, Saka became one of Arsenal's top assist providers, highlighting his creativity on the field.
- ⚽ European Competitions: Saka has represented Arsenal

in various European competitions, including the UEFA Europa League, gaining valuable experience.

⚽   International Recognition: His performances for Arsenal led to his call-up to the England national team, where he continued to impress on the international stage.

⚽   Developed Under Arteta: Saka's growth as a player has

been significantly influenced by Mikel Arteta, Arsenal's manager, who has helped him hone his skills.

⚽   High Market Value: Due to his consistent performances, Saka's market value has risen significantly, reflecting his importance in the football world.

⚽   Key to Arsenal's Attack: Saka has become a crucial component of Arsenal's attacking play, known for his pace, dribbling, and creativity.

⚽   Loyal to Arsenal: Despite interest from other clubs, Saka has remained loyal to Arsenal, expressing his commitment to the club's future.

⚽   Named to Premier League Team of the Year: Saka's outstanding performances earned him a spot in the Premier League Team of the

Year, acknowledging his contributions.

- ⚽ Multiple Awards: Apart from club honours, Saka has received individual awards for his performances, reinforcing his status as a rising star.
- ⚽ Influence on Young Players: As a young and successful footballer, Saka has become an inspiration to aspiring players in Arsenal's academy and beyond.

NATIONAL TEAM CAREER

- ⚽ England Debut: Bukayo Saka made his debut for the England national team on 7 October 2020 in a friendly against Wales, marking the beginning of his senior international career.
- ⚽ First Goal: His first goal for England came against Austria in a warm-up match for Euro

2020, a significant milestone in his international career.

- ⚽ Euro 2020 Squad: Saka was selected for the England squad at Euro 2020, where he played a crucial role in the team's journey to the final.
- ⚽ Youngest England Player in a Major Final: Saka became the youngest player ever to represent England in a major final during Euro 2020, showing his early impact.

- ⚽ Penalty Shootout in Euro 2020 Final: Saka's penalty miss in the Euro 2020 final shootout against Italy was a defining moment, but he received widespread support from fans and players.
- ⚽ Versatile National Team Role: Saka has played in various positions for England, including left-back and right-wing, demonstrating his

versatility at the international level.

⚽ England's Young Talent: He is considered one of England's brightest young talents, with a promising future ahead in the national team.

⚽ World Cup 2022 Selection: Saka was selected for England's squad for the 2022 FIFA World Cup in Qatar, highlighting his consistent performances for the national team.

⚽ Impactful Performances: Saka has consistently delivered impactful performances for England, contributing goals and assists in key matches.

⚽ International Recognition: His performances for England have earned him recognition on the international stage, with praise from football analysts and fans.

⚽   Fastest England Goal: Saka holds the record for scoring one of the fastest goals for England, demonstrating his quick reflexes and goal-scoring ability.

⚽   Young Player Awards: Saka has received various young player awards for his performances with England, underscoring his rising star status.

- ⚽ Regular National Team Call-Ups: Saka has become a regular call-up for the England national team, reflecting his growing importance in the squad.
- ⚽ Positive Relationship with Gareth Southgate: Saka has a positive relationship with England manager Gareth Southgate, who has helped

him develop at the international level.

- ⚽ Collaborations with England Teammates: Saka's partnerships with other England players, such as Harry Kane and Raheem Sterling, have been instrumental in England's success.
- ⚽ Goal-Scoring Ability: Saka's ability to score goals for England from various

positions has made him a valuable asset to the national team.

⚽   Team Spirit and Camaraderie: Saka is known for his positive attitude and camaraderie with his England teammates, contributing to the team's strong spirit.

⚽   Continued Development: Saka continues to improve and develop as a national team player, aiming to become one of England's leading players in the future.

- ⚽ Inspiration for Young Footballers: His success with the England national team has inspired many young footballers in the UK to pursue their dreams.
- ⚽ Commitment to England: Despite his Nigerian heritage, Saka has committed to representing England at the international level,

demonstrating his loyalty to the Three Lions.

RECORDS AND PERSONAL ACHIEVEMENTS

⚽ High Market Value: Bukayo Saka's current market value is €130.00 million, reflecting his status as one of the most valuable young players in world football.

⚽ Youngest England Player in Major Final: Saka became the youngest player to represent England in a major final during the Euro 2020 final against Italy, showcasing his talent on the international stage.

- ⚽ Arsenal's Player of the Season: He was named Arsenal's Player of the Season in 2020-2021, underlining his impact on the club at a young age.
- ⚽ Record for Penalty Conversion: Saka has

achieved an impressive record for penalty conversions, demonstrating his calmness under pressure.

- ⚽ Consistent Performances: Saka's consistent performances in the Premier League have made him one of the most reliable players for Arsenal and a regular in the starting lineup.
- ⚽ First-Team Appearances: Saka has made over 100 first-

team appearances for Arsenal, a significant milestone considering his age.

⚽   International Caps: He has earned 32 caps for the England national team, scoring 11 goals, illustrating his rapid rise in international football.

⚽   Top Assists Provider: Saka has become one of Arsenal's top assists providers, showcasing his ability to create scoring opportunities for his teammates.

- ⚽ Contract Extension with Arsenal: Saka's long-term contract extension with Arsenal until 2027 shows the club's commitment to his development and future.
- ⚽ Honours and Awards: Saka has won several honours with Arsenal, including the FA Cup in 2019-2020 and two FA

Community Shields in 2020 and 2023, as well as being awarded Premier League Player of the Month in March 2023.

TECHNIQUE AND PLAYING STYLE

⚽ Agility and Footwork: Bukayo Saka's agility and quick footwork set him apart, allowing him to swiftly manoeuvre around defenders and create scoring opportunities.

⚽ Versatility: Saka is a highly versatile player, capable of performing in multiple positions, including left-back, left-wing, and right-wing, which reflects his adaptability on the pitch.

⚽ Dribbling Skills: His dribbling techniques are exceptional, with the ability to take on defenders with ease, showcasing his control and creativity.

⚽ Intelligence on the Field: Saka is known for his football intelligence, often making smart decisions in high-pressure situations and finding the right passes.

- ⚽ Crossing Ability: His crossing ability is a key asset, providing accurate deliveries into the box for teammates to capitalise on.
- ⚽ Creativity and Vision: Saka's creativity and vision allow him to see opportunities others might

miss, making him a constant threat in the attacking third.

- ⚽   Physical Strength: Despite his agility, Saka also possesses a surprising level of physical strength, enabling him to hold off defenders and maintain possession.
- ⚽   Technical Skills: Saka has a high level of technical skill, with precise ball control and a decisive stride that makes him a standout performer.

- ⚽ Calm Under Pressure: He is known for remaining calm under pressure, even in crucial moments, which adds to his reliability as a player.
- ⚽ Goal-Scoring Instincts: Saka has a natural goal-scoring instinct, often finding the back of the net from various positions, demonstrating his clinical finishing.

Made in the USA
Columbia, SC
14 July 2024

38612451R00030